EXCUSE ME GOD...

WHAT DID YOU SAY?

HOW TO RECOGNISE THE VOICE OF GOD

BY

ANTHONY ESENWA

Cover design by Adeola Disu www.creataa.com

Published in the United Kingdom

Published by Sichys Publishing
info@sichyspublishing.com
www.sichyspublishing.com

DEDICATION

To Daniel and Emmanuel Esenwa,
the two arrows in my quiver.

Contents

INTRODUCTION

Being able to hear God and recognise what he is saying, or showing, is a very important aspect of our spiritual journey. There are many people today who are able to hear and understand what God has said to them and are finding fulfillment in their walk with God, or at least having the assurance of the guidance of The One who knows all things and is able to see what lies in the future. Every lover of God should desire to, not only hear from God, but also recognise what God is saying.

There are many people, including preachers, who think and teach that it is impossible to hear from God today as people did in Bible times. Some of them may have been taught all their lives that they do not qualify to hear from God and therefore do not make efforts to prepare themselves or learn how God communicates to people. The scripture is full of verses were God promised to be with and lead His people. God's method of leading his people is by speaking or showing something to them. God will not shove us around like robots to do things, even though they may be good for us and others. He will say or show things to people who carry out what they understand of God's instructions. That empowerment to hear or receive from God is what the book tries to help the reader attain. The knowledge from this book can be the missing link that helps you take your relationship with God to the next level of intimacy.

It is possible that you already hear or see but do not understand that it is God communicating with you. This book will explore 12 ways God has reached out to people in the past and is still using to communicate with people today.

My hope is that reading this book will make a big difference to your relationship with God and contribute towards your finding guidance and fulfillment in your journey here in this world.

Anthony Esenwa

30th April, 2024.

CHAPTER 1

GOD STILL SPEAKS TO PEOPLE TODAY

Your ears shall hear a word behind you, saying, "This is the way, walk in it," Whenever you turn to the right hand, or whenever you turn to the left.
– Isaiah 30:21 (NKJV)

A few years ago, I travelled to Cardiff from Northern England to see if I can move over to live there. I had prayed about the journey before setting off and during my prayers the Lord had told me that He will be with me. When I got there, I needed a place to stay for the night. I walked into a phone booth and prayed, asking the Lord to provide me a place as I knew that He was with me on the journey.

As I was praying, I felt something like a tap on my shoulder and heard a voice that said "Follow me!" I came out of the phone booth and started walking in the direction the voice was leading me. I walked around 200 meters along the road and the voice said "Turn left" and I did, and kept walking. After a while I heard "Turn left" again, and I did. I got to a pub (that is public house where people go to drink and socialise) which also had a 'Bed and Breakfast' facility. I went in there and while speaking to the pub landlady about a room for the night, a gentleman came and offered me a place in another building just opposite the pub. It was a nice, clean and warm room and I stayed there for the night. A few weeks later when I moved to live in Cardiff I lived in that same house. God led me there in a city where I knew no one and provided a place for me. This is just one example of how God can speak to and lead us when we're in need.

God still speaks to people today unveiling His plans for our lives and leading us out of difficulties.

If you are a believer in God and do not hear from Him, you are missing out on one of the best gifts of God; the great advantage of being guided by Him. He promised in many areas of the scriptures to lead and guide you, and if you do not hear when He is directing you how can He then guide you?

I believe that there has to be an advantage of having the Spirit of God in a person's life and one the advantages is being led by Him. The Bible tells us that God's Spirit searches all things and reveals them to us.

> *But God has revealed them to us through His Spirit. For the Spirit searches all things, yes, the deep things of God. - 1 Cor 2:10 (NKJV)*

Many people, including some church leaders, teach that God no longer speaks to people today as He did in the past. They preach and teach from their own limitations and make it look like God has changed. They teach about how God spoke to Noah, Abraham, Moses and the prophets and yet say that those days are past and that God does not speak any more. They make it look like God has changed and that the Bible should not be truly believed. Yet there may be people sitting right there in the congregation thinking that there must be more to being a nominal church goer. They are yearning to experience something different, to hear God's voice or just have an encounter with or experience God in a deeper way. In order to receive what the Spirit of God is revealing it is important to believe that He still speaks to people today and expect to hear from Him. How can anyone receive from God or know what is revealed if they do not believe that God still speaks to people today?

If you really long to hear from God, you can right now if you listen or if you know how He communicates. God is speaking to people right now and may have even reached out to you.

CHAPTER 2

WHY MAY GOD SPEAK TO YOU?

Surely the Lord GOD does nothing,
Unless He reveals His secret to His
servants the prophets.
– Amos 3:7 (NKJV)

There are very many reasons why God would want to speak to an individual or group. To understand why God would want to speak to you, it's important to try to view the world or the whole of creation from God's perspective; to see the bigger picture of the world and things around you.

There's a tendency to be locked into our own desires, needs and worries, and have a narrow-minded view of things. We can sometimes think that the world is all about us; our provisions, protection, happiness etc., and forget about other people or other creations of God. When God speaks to people it may be about their own personal matter or about matters that concern others, a group or society, or even the world. We shall consider some reasons why God may want to speak to a person.

About You and Your Affairs

God is always willing to guide and lead us to the ultimate happiness in life, and He does this by speaking to us continually. If God gave you every single detailed instruction to make your life happy and fulfilling, you are likely to forget most of it before long. He reveals His plans to us gradually and in piecemeal. This is important so that we are able to follow one step at a time. If all of God's instructions came, all at once, the world will become a chaotic place as many people will do things randomly and out of order and in some cases, placing the cart before the horse, doing last things first and first things last. God speaks to us from time to time to help us achieve that ultimate happiness and fulfilment one step at a time.

Many people today experience the leading and direction of God to do things or abstain from things, and find that leading them to safety or something positive in their lives. God's voice or leading also comes when we go through difficult times to comfort and guide us or bring solutions to ordinary life issues.

A Christian sister once told me that she had a particular skin issue and had some medical treatments but the issue remained, and so she started praying about it. One day as she was driving, she heard a gentle voice in her heart telling her to stop eating a certain type of nut. She did as she was told and the skin issue cleared out; her skin was restored. She got her healing or solution by first recognizing that she heard from God and then doing what she was told. We read from the prophecy of Isaiah that;

> *And though the Lord gives you the bread of adversity and the water of affliction, yet your teachers will not be moved into a corner anymore, but your eyes shall see your teachers. Your ears shall hear a word behind*

> *you, saying, "This is the way, walk in it,"*
> *Whenever you turn to the right hand or*
> *whenever you turn to the left. (NKJV) —*
> *Isaiah 30:20.*

This is God's promise to continually lead us by his voice; "your ears shall hear a word behind you..." God's word may come whether you are prepared for it or not, but recognizing it will depend on what you know about hearing from God and how prepared you are.

When God speaks to a person to save them out of personal trouble or danger it is part of His big plan to save or lead *all of creation* to the ultimate good.

About other People and the World

It is important to remember that God made all things including all peoples from every language, kingdom and nation, and that He wants the well-being of all. God may speak to you or someone regarding something that affects other people, society or the world. The Bible is a good example of this. In the Bible we read about how God speaks to people individually or to families, nations and the whole world. Some of the things He says to an individual or nation can apply to others because God does not change.

> *For I am the LORD, I do not change...*
> *-- Malachi 3:6 (NKJV)*

And what I say to you, I say to all ...
— Mark 13:37 (NKJV)

God wants the salvation of the whole of creation, and salvation here means attaining the ultimate good or perfection. Creation cannot save itself or guide itself to perfection, only God can truly save creation. God sends His word to steer creation towards that perfect good. So, when God speaks to a person, it may be for people in places unknown to the person, but that person becomes an instrument for the greater good.

God's Will on Earth

One other main reason God speaks to people is to establish His Will on the earth. When the will of God is done on the Earth then the Kingdom of God is truly come.

What is the will of God? We learn from the scriptures that God's will on the earth is mainly two pronged:

1. Establish a perfect relationship between God and people. This means the true knowledge of God in holiness, reverence and love.

2. Establish a perfect relationship among people everywhere. This involves love of other people, fairness, justice and righteous living.

Many times, God speaks to people about things happening to other people or places, or events that will happen in the future. God does this because the whole world belongs to Him, and throughout the ages He has confided in people, revealing future events to them. There are many instances in scriptures where God, or through His agents, reveals future events to people like the birth of children, destinies of people and nations, and worldwide events.

For example, many years before the flood in the book of Genesis, God spoke to Noah telling him to prepare for it and build an ark to save mankind and animals from extinction. God also told Abraham that he will have many children long before he had the first one. The Bible book of Revelation is focused on future events affecting the early church and many nations, including events in the spiritual realm, and life beyond how we know it on earth.

This perspective of the world as a whole and as all belonging to the Almighty God will help us comprehend why God may want to speak to us about places we have never been or people we have never met, or even people we do not like.

CHAPTER 3

DOES GOD SPEAK TO SINNERS?

*For all have sinned and fall short of
the glory of God.
— Roman 3:23 (NKJV)*

It is important to consider this question as many people discount themselves from benefiting anything from God due to self-inflicted sense of guilt. I also want to deal with the question as it can sometimes be the cause of debate among many religious people.

Taking sin to mean offence against God, it will be correct to say that most, if not all, human beings have sinned against God and continue to do so.

> *For all have sinned and fall short of the glory of God.*
> *– Roman 3:23 (NKJV)*

However, in this context, we refer to a sinner as anyone who knowingly continues to offend God and makes no effort to repent. In order to determine if and how God may speak to sinners requires a good understanding of the different ways in which God may speak or communicate with people. How we hear God or receive what is communicated depends on how the communication is initiated.

Let us start by thinking about how we communicate with the people around us. We will consider two main ways of initiating communication; one is initiated to give information and the other is initiated to ask questions.

In the first method of initiating communication, the receiver or hearer does not necessarily have to do anything and may not even be listening but they may still hear or receive. Then their attention is drawn to the point being made or the object of communication. This is a very common way of communicating with people or things around us and God uses this method too.

In this first way, God initiates the communication and the hearer or the called does not necessarily have to do anything to prepare them for the communication. We see this method of communication in many parts of the Bible where people were not prepared or have to qualify in any way to hear from God or His agents. Moses' encounter with God is a good example of how a person can just be about their normal life and God reaches out to that person.

> *Now Moses was tending the flock of Jethro his father-in-law, the priest of Midian. And he led the flock to the back of the desert, and came to Horeb, the mountain of God. And the Angel of the LORD appeared to him in a flame of fire from the midst of a bush. So he looked, and behold, the bush was burning with fire, but the bush was not consumed. Then Moses said, "I will now turn aside and see this great sight, why the bush does not burn." So when the LORD*

> *saw that he turned aside to look, God called*
> *to him from the midst of the bush and said,*
> *"Moses, Moses!" And he said, "Here I*
> *am." - Exodus 3:1-4 (NKJV)*

The second way in which communication is initiated is in the form of enquiry or question in which the person needing information initiates it. In this second method, communication is dependent on the disposition of the other to be complete. If there's no good relationship or disposition, a response may not be given. We see an example in this psalm attributed to David where he laments that his request seems to go unanswered:

> *My God, my God, why have you forsaken*
> *me? Why are you so far from saving me, so*
> *far from my cries of anguish? My God, I*
> *cry out by day, but you do not answer, by*
> *night, but I find no rest.*
> *- Psalm 22:1-2 (NIV)*

In the first way, God initiates the communication and He speaks to anyone including sinners, and does that directly or indirectly through various means. The Bible, for instance, contains God's message to everyone whether they are righteous or wicked. There are many examples in the Bible where God initiated a conversation or sent a message to those considered sinners or wicked. God sent the prophet Ahijah to speak to King Jerobaom through the king's wife (1

Kings 14:5-16), and specifically told him:

> *"but you have done more evil than all who were before you." - NKJV (1 Kings 14:9)*

Jeroboam may have been a sinner, a wicked king but God still spoke to him through a prophet.

CHAPTER 4

12 WAYS GOD CAN SPEAK TO YOU

"And it shall come to pass afterward That I will pour out My Spirit on all flesh; Your sons and your daughters shall prophesy, Your old men shall dream dreams, Your young men shall see visions..."
– Joel 2:28 (NKJV)

There are many ways in which God can speak or communicate with us. Understanding these modes of communication can help us recognise or comprehend what God is saying. Here are Twelve different ways in which God communicated with people in the Bible and which He can use to reach us today.

Face to Face

The context of Face to face here means an intimate and direct communication with God. In Exodus chapter 33 and verse 11 we read that God spoke to Moses, as a person would speak to another; face to face. God also confirmed that He spoke, face to face, with Moses in Numbers 12:7-8.

The Bible account of the interaction between the first people in the world (Adam and Eve) and God, suggests that they talked with God face to face. In Genesis chapter 3 we get the sense that God talked with Adam and his wife, Eve, directly. In verse 8 (Genesis 3:8) they heard the sound of God walking in the garden and they went to hide. This suggests that they knew the difference between being in God's presence and hiding from God.

God spoke to people in that way in the past and can

choose to do so again today. God may choose to speak to people face to face now; it is not impossible but the choice is God's choice and not ours.

Visions

Vision in this context is a spiritual experience in which the visioner receives pictorial message or communications of events as if they are happening before them, either in a flash or over a period. This means the visioners sees spiritual things or events as if looking at pictures or seeing a movie. Visions can be about past, present or future events, they can last from split seconds to hours and days.

There are many people in the Bible who saw or had the experience of visions; a very notable one is the author of the book of Revelation, almost the whole book is about the visions he saw.

God speaks to many people today through visions. In Joel 2:28 God promised to enable people to see visions:

> *And it shall come to pass afterward, that I will pour out my spirit upon all flesh; and your sons and your daughters shall prophesy, your old men shall dream dreams, your young men shall see visions – Joel 2:28 (KJV)*

Through visions we see what God wants us to see about issues that concern us, other people or nations and the world. Through the medium of vision, we see God's message in pictures.

Dreams

People across many cultures believe that dreams are very important ways of knowing what happens in the spirit world, or receiving a message from the spiritual realm about the past, present or future. Dreams are similar to visions but the difference is that they generally happen when a person is sleeping. God speaks to many people in dreams.

There are examples in the Bible of people having life changing encounters or receiving messages in dreams. Joseph for example had a dream that we now know means that he will be exalted above his parents and brothers and that they will bow to him. Joseph's first dream is recorded in Genesis 37:5-7, the second dream is in Genesis 37:9

> *Then he dreamed still another dream and told it to his brothers, and said, "Look, I have dreamed another dream. And this time, the sun, the moon, and the eleven stars bowed down to me." – NKJV (Genesis 37:9)*

We know from the life of Joseph that he became the

ruler of Egypt, and only Pharaoh King of Egypt, was greater than Joseph when he ruled.

Dreams are important ways of hearing from God directly or through His agents, and because they are involuntary, they can generally be trusted as a way of hearing from God. We also note that dreams can result from many circumstances or sources such as traumas, fears, past events or from demons and evil powers. However, we need to understand that God has spoken to people in the past through dreams and is still speaking to many today by the same means.

Inner Witness

Inner witness comes as an impression inside of us leading us to be convinced about something or a decision. Inner witness can sometimes manifest as a gentle or strong impression. This method of communicating with us is quite common and some people refer to it as a hunch. We may hear people say that "Something inside me told me…" It is important to mention here that there can be many 'voices' or 'impressions' that people hear or get from different sources and for various reasons so it should not be taken that every strong impression or hunch is from God. You can be wrong a few times due to your own personal emotions and desires but practice can help you know the difference between what God is saying and where your emotion is leading.

This method of hearing God can be improved through prayers and meditations. I personally became conscious of this method of hearing God when I became aware of that gentle inner certainty. I started asking God, and listening within me for answers, before doing certain things or making certain decision. I would then make a note of what I am convinced I heard through the inner witness and compare it with the actual outcome. Doing this several times helped me differentiate my emotions and desires from what God is saying to me.

Through Other People

This method involves God speaking to people through intermediaries. God speaks to people through other people. You may find yourself in a situation, desperate for an answer or solution about something that you have been praying for and God brings someone who says something that answers your question or gives you the solution. This person may be a stranger or someone you know, maybe a friend, leader or just a passer-by. God can use anybody to speak to you.

It can also happen that the person God sends knows that they have been sent to you and they may say that God sent them. We have examples of God sending people to speak to others in the Bible, God sent Ahijah to Jeroboam through his wife.

> *And so it was, when Ahijah heard the sound*
> *of her footsteps as she came through the door,*
> *he said, "Come in, wife of Jeroboam. Why*
> *do you pretend to be another person? For I*
> *have been sent to you with bad news. Go, tell*
> *Jeroboam, 'Thus says the Lord God…'*
> *— 1 Kings 14:6-7 (NKJV)*

God may want to use other people to let you know that the message is from Him. God may send other people to say things to you that only you would have known so that you can believe that it is from Him. The message from other people can come as a confirmation of what God has already told you through other way of hearing from Him such as visions, inner witness, dreams etc.

Prophecy

This is a unique way of God speaking through a person to people which can be instantaneous or over time. Here God uses special people anointed or appointed to do that special task. This is similar to the section, just above, where we considered the method of God speaking to us through other people. However, this method is different in that a prophet or prophetess is specially anointed or appointed for that position or duty. The prophet becomes a vessel or instrument of communication at that time. They may sometimes want to stop speaking but find that they cannot stop until the message is completely delivered. The Bible is full of prophetic messages from God to certain individuals, nations and future generations like us today.

> *I have also sent to you all My servants the prophets, rising up early and sending them, saying, 'Turn now everyone from his evil way, amend your doings, and do not go after other gods to serve them; then you will dwell in the land which I have given you and your fathers.' But you have not inclined your ear, nor obeyed Me.*
> *– Jeremiah 35:15 (NKJV)*

Audible Voice

This is a method where a person hears audible voices as though they were in conversation with someone although they do not see who is speaking. God spoke to people in the past through audible voices and I believe that He is still speaking to many today in the same way. We understand that in the wilderness, God spoke to the Hebrews in audible voices and the sound of thunder. When Jesus was transfigured before Peter and John, they heard the audible voice of God on the mount of transfiguration.

> *…when such a voice came to Him from the Excellent Glory: "This is My beloved Son, in whom I am well pleased." And we heard*

> *this voice which came from heaven when we were with Him on the holy mountain. - 1 Peter 1:18 (NKJV)*

We also read from the Bible that God spoke to the boy Samuel as he laid in the Tabernacle. The call was audible so the boy ran to Eli thinking it was Eli who called him. This happened three times before Eli understood that it was The Lord calling the boy. Read the full account in 1 Samuel 3:1-10.

The first time I heard an audible voice, I was about eighteen years old. I had read that a person's spirit can come out of their body and return back into the body through meditation. My young mind was fascinated by the thought of coming out of my body and looking at things from that different perspective so I decided to try it. I sat on a chair in our living room, positioned myself in meditation and after a while, I don't remember how long, I heard my name called out audibly and loud. I was sure that the voice was from within the room but when I opened my eyes there was no one with me there. In that experience I felt like there was another presence in the room but I didn't see anybody, I felt afraid and stopped the meditation. It was a very memorable experience for me and one that will be difficult to forget.

God can speak to anyone He chooses, anywhere He chooses and anyway He chooses including in audible voice.

Through Angels

God sends angels as intermediaries to communicate His message to a person or people. Angels are spiritual agents who act on God's behalf or serve as His messengers.

There is a well-known Bible account of an Angel with a messenger is in Luke 1:26-38. In that account God sent the angel Gabriel to tell Mary that she will be the mother of Jesus who will be called the Son of the Most High. The young Mary had questions about how it will happen and the angel explained that the Holy Spirit will make it happen. The same angel Gabriel was also sent to Zachariah to announce the birth of John the Baptist in Luke 1: 11-20. There are many other examples of angels bringing God's messages to people in Bible times. God sent angels to Abraham, Moses, Daniel, Peter and John (the author of the Book of Revelation) and many others.

This angelic method of God reaching out to people usually presents opportunities to ask questions, get explanations about messages and information about other things that are not part of the core message. There is an example of this in the account of the angel that appeared to Daniel after his three weeks of fasting and prayers (Daniel 10:10-21).

Daniel was fasting and praying, and twenty-one days into his prayers, an angel appeared to him bringing a message in response to his prayers. The angel explains that he had been sent in response to Daniel's from the first day of his prayer but he was delayed in some kind of fight or resistance by the 'Prince of Persia, which sounds like a spiritual territorial agent over that part of the world, and it took the intervention of another angel called Michael, 'one of the chief princes,' to let this messenger angel get through to Daniel.

We learn from this angel that; there are spiritual authorities over territories, that angel Michael is a higher authority, and we also get an insight into what happens in the spiritual realm when we pray. We now know how messages and answers to prayers can travel from God to us through angels, and the conflicts that occur in the spiritual realm while we humans are obliviously going about our businesses.

God has sent me several angels with different messages at different times, some gave their names when I asked along with their principal duties. God can send you an angel with a message today if He thinks it necessary or if you ask. The Bible tells us in Psalm 34:7 that the angel of the Lord encamps around the children of God. There may be an angel with you now and you can initiate a conversation with that angel if you prepare, speak and listen for what that angel may say.

Through Signs

God speaks to people through signs. This is when God sends or shows a sign to reveal, confirm or validate something. Moses' encounter with the 'burning bush' is a popular example of a sign from God. Here the Bible describes how Moses saw a bush in flames and yet not burning as it should be expected. Then curiosity drew him near to the bush. Through that sign and others, he became convinced that he was actually encountering the God of Abraham, Isaac and Jacob. Moses was emboldened by those signs and wonders to go back to Egypt, confront Pharaoh and save his people out of the bondage of slavery.

Another good example is that of Gideon, an angel of the Lord appeared to Gideon in Judges 6:1-20. The angel told Gideon that God was going to use him to deliver His people. He asked the angel for a sign to really prove that this message was from God. Gideon was given the sign that empowered and emboldened him to do what the angel told him and he became victorious against all odds.

Signs and wonders from God give us courage and impetus to act or do what we believe God is telling us to do. This method of God speaking to us is very powerful and it can remove fear and doubt, fill us with certainty and increase our faith in the area God is speaking to us. You too can ask God for a sign today and He will give you one or more. He communicated with many people and prophets through signs and wonders and will give you a sign if you ask. God also told Jeremiah to "Ask of me and I will show you thing you don't know " (Jeremiah 33.3)

In Isaiah, God said,

> *"I will lift up an ensign and whistle…"*
> *-- Isaiah 5:26 (NKJV)*

Through Animals

In this method God uses animals to speak to people. This is to show that He is Lord over all creation - man and beast alike. A good example of this is the story of Balam in Numbers 22:21-39.

Balaam was going to do something that was not pleasing to God even after he had been warned not to. An angel stood on the way to stop the donkey on which he was riding. Balaam struck the donkey to get it to move and the donkey spoke. This seems like an extreme case where God uses something unheard-of or unthinkable to emphasize His message to Balaam.

Inspired Words and Songs

This method of God communicating to us is quite subtle and easily missed by many. This is when God, through His Spirit, brings to our consciousness, certain information that is already in us but stored away somewhere in our minds just like data stored in a computer memory or hard drive. This can be in the form of words or songs that jumps out of us, and bearing answers to questions that we have or new information from God. This is comparable to what

Jesus describes in Matthew 13:52;

> *… like the owner of a house who brings out of his storeroom new treasures as well as old.*
> *-- Matthew 13: 52 (NKJV)*

I had a dream some time ago, and in that dream, I saw a church usher or steward being unduly harsh with a child in an attempt to correct that child. Then I heard a voice say; Faithfulness must go with kindness. I woke up from that dream with a song by Glen Campell which I heard many years ago with the lyrics;

> *You've got to try a little kindness*
> *Yes, show a little kindness*
> *Just shine your light for everyone to see*
> *And if you try a little kindness*
> *Then you'll overlook the blindness*
> *Of narrow-minded people on the narrow-minded streets*

The Lord taught me from that dream that people have to do what they have a duty to do, but their faithfulness to duty must be accompanied with kindness. I learnt this message, not only from the dream, but also from information (in this case a song) that I heard many years before, which was stored away somewhere in my subconscious.

It may be that a song or words you heard some time ago just keeps coming back to your consciousness continuously. Pay attention to the meaning of the words or song, God may be saying something to you.

The Bible

The Bible is a very important way God speaks to us. The Bible is an inspired book which has come to us through several authors all inspired by the Holy Spirit. It is a collection of texts over thousands of years which still tells us the truth and plans of God for us today.

Every time we read the bible through the eyes of faith we are inspired and God reveals new things to us. The Bible tells us the plans and personality of God and is also the sure standard of a wise and happy living. Since God does not change, we can rely on what He said to people in Bible times to still be relevant to us today.

How Does God Speak Through The Bible?

1. God speaks to us as we read what He said to various people in Bible times. What He said to people in the past is what He will say to us in similar circumstances. When God spoke the commandments to Moses, He told him to write the commandments so that future generations can read and keep them.

2. People are inspired by Bible passages which speaks about situations similar to theirs and answer their questions or solve their dilemmas.

3. If a person believes that they have heard God through other means like dreams, visions, prophecy etc., the Bible can be the standard against which they verify what they have heard

4. God's word in the Bible can bring us comfort, strength and healing.

5. The Bible corrects and rebukes us where necessary, as though God himself was telling us how to conduct our lives.

CHAPTER 5

RECOGNISING WHAT GOD IS SAYING

"The whole vision has become to you like the words of a book that is sealed, which men deliver to one who is literate, saying, "Read this, please." And he says, "I cannot, for it is sealed." Then the book is delivered to one who is illiterate, saying, "Read this, please." And he says, "I am not literate."
– Isaiah 29:11-12 (NKJV)

Many people already hear or receive from God but do not understand and cannot make sense of what is communicated to them. The essence of communication is to send or exchange and understand information, thoughts or emotions between individuals or among parties. Hearing or receiving from God will not do much good if what is communicated is not understood or is misunderstood.

God can sometimes communicate with a person or group in what may seem like their local language but many times God speaks to people in symbols, parables and metaphors. This can be difficult for the unprepared to understand or make sense of. There are many examples of people who heard from God and completely misunderstood what was said. The Apostles of Jesus were in that situation many times.

One time Jesus was warning the disciples to *"…beware of the yeast of the Pharisees and Sadducees"* (Matthew 16:5-12) and they misunderstood what he meant probably because he used the word 'yeast'; they thought he was talking about bread. After he explained they then understood that he was warning them against the "teaching of the Pharisees and Sadducees". This is the case with many people today.

In many cultures around the world people speak in proverbs or parables and the stranger or the unlearned cannot make sense of what is being said unless it is explained to them. God's message to us comes in that way many times. Just as it is written in Isaiah 29:11-12 (NKJV)

> *"The whole vision has become to you like the words of a book that is sealed, which men deliver to one who is literate, saying, "Read this, please." And he says, "I cannot, for it is sealed." Then the book is delivered to one who is illiterate, saying, "Read this, please." And he says, "I am not literate."*
> *- Isaiah 29:11-12 (NKJV)*

Interpreting God's message involves a combination of personal dispositions, faith, spiritual understanding and preparedness.

Faith

> *But without faith it is impossible to please Him, for he who comes to God must believe that He is, and that He is a rewarder of those who diligently seek Him.*
> *— Hebrews 11:6 (NKJV)*

Faith, that is expression of belief in God, is very important in any relationship with God. In other to understand what God is saying, you must first believe that God is, otherwise how can you understand if you don't believe that the One speaking exists. You cannot be undecided and receive anything from God. You have to be definite and resolute in your belief in God.

The presence of doubt, which is lack of faith, can create internal noises that is capable of drowning out the message God is sending to you. Faith is therefore foundational to hearing and understanding God, it also makes you open and receptive to messages from Him.

Humility and Openness

The pride of your heart has deceived you, you who dwell in the clefts of the rock, whose habitation is high… - Obadiah 1:3 (NKJV)

Humility and openness are very important in building a good understanding of how God speaks and how we understand what He is communicating. Pride is deceptive and can make you think you know when you do not. Being humble can help us open our mind to possibilities and discover new and deep meanings in the symbolic or metaphoric language of God. God interacts with people in different ways and cannot be restricted to one way of doing things.

Recognising that our understanding is limited can enable us keep open minds, learn from research and other people as well as grow in our relationship with

God thereby improving our spiritual understanding.

Prayer and Meditation

'Call to Me, and I will answer you, and show you great and mighty things, which you do not know.'
– Jeremiah 33:3 (NKJV)

Through prayer and meditation, we speak to God and also get in touch with ourselves. In prayer, we talk and listen to God while in meditation we are in touch with ourselves, the environment and the presence of God. Our world can be very distracting and fill us with lots of internal noises, but through meditation and prayer we can train our minds and spirits towards quietness and tranquility so we can hear ourselves and distinguish other spiritual voices.

Regular prayers and meditations help us attune our minds and heart to God and grow in our relationship with Him. As we grow in our relationship with God, we understand what He is saying better. God spoke to Jeremiah saying *"Call upon me and I will answer you and show you…"* (Jeremiah 33:3). This means that if we reach out to God, He will reach out to us. Through regular prayer and meditation, we are enabled by the Holy Spirit to understand God's messages better.

Fellowship with other Believers

*As iron sharpens iron, so a man sharpens
the countenance of his friend.
-- Proverbs 27:17 (NKJV)*

Fellowship with other believers helps spiritual growth and maturity, which in turn helps us understand spiritual experiences and insights. It provides us the platform to share experiences and interpretations with other believers which can contribute to a collective understanding of supernatural communication.

Spiritual Guidance

Seeking guidance is very important in any spiritual endeavor including hearing from and understanding what God is saying. Get spiritual direction or advice from a trusted, proven and mature Christian leader who is filled with the Spirit of God and can provide guidance in understanding and interpreting God's message. Be careful of people who claim to be what they are not. Do not get spiritual guidance from people who do not believe that God can speak to you as they may lead you to confusion or cause you to doubt that you even heard from God.

Personal Discernment

This is developing your own way of understanding and distinguishing spiritual voices or experiences.

Reflecting on your own circumstances, experiences and emotions in the light of spiritual teachings and the Bible can help you develop discernment. As you grow in your spiritual maturity, you become more adept at recognizing what God is saying to you.

Understanding Cultural and Historical Context

Language is part of culture so it is crucial to have a good understanding of the cultural and historical context of symbolic messages God may be sending you. Learn the symbolic meanings in your own culture, and then those of Bible times as this can aid interpretation. Many cultures have phrases, idioms, proverbs, parables or figures of speech that carry more meaning than their direct transliteration. Many people in Bible times misunderstood Jesus because he frequently spoke to them in parables and you can misunderstand God if you do not understand symbolic language.

Understanding what God is saying is an ongoing process and every believer needs to continue to deepen their relationship with God and constantly seek to understand how He speaks to them. One believer may find a different meaning to what God is saying based on their unique approach and spiritual journeys.

CHAPTER 6

SPIRITUAL DISCERNMENT

"Beloved do not believe every spirit, but test the spirits, whether they are of God; because many false prophets have gone out into the world"
— 1 John 4:1 (NKJV)

Interacting with God in any way is a spiritual or supernatural experience and is not usually empirically verified. While it is possible to physically verify the outcome of what God has told a person, it is not usually possible to scientifically measure or empirically prove that God spoke to that person.

For instance, if God tells you that your first child will be a girl and it happens as He said, people can see the result but there is no scientific way to prove that God said so. This then means that spiritual or supernatural encounters are only spiritually discerned or understood usually through the eyes of faith.

Just as we know that God speaks to people, we also know that there are many other voices or sources of spiritual information. A person may be hearing themselves as a result of their own desires and may try to convince themselves and others that they have heard from God.

Supernatural and spiritual means of information and communication such as visions, dreams, prophecies and others can come from various sources including demons and powers of darkness. It is important to identify the sources of communication to ensure that one does not fall into the trap of deception. It is quite easy to get carried away with our thoughts, emotions and desires, mistaking them to be voice of God.

We read, in Act of Apostle chapter 16 from verse 16 to 18, about a slave girl who had the spirit of divination which could have been mistaken for the spirit of God.

> *One day as we were going to the place of prayer, we were met by a slave girl with a spirit of divination, who earned a large income for her masters by fortune-telling. This girl followed Paul and the rest of us, shouting, "These men are servants of the Most High God, who are proclaiming to you the way of salvation!" She continued this for many days. Eventually Paul grew so aggravated that he turned and said to the spirit, "In the name of Jesus Christ I command you to come out of her!" And the spirit left her at that very moment.*

Notice that the slave girl was not particularly saying evil things about Paul and his group but she did not have the spirit of God. When Paul rebuked the spirit in the name of Jesus it left the girl. People may say things that sound good but may be saying them by evil powers. Do not be deceived and carried away.

1 John 4:1 admonishes us to:

> *…not believe every spirit, but test the spirits, whether they are of God; because many false*

prophets have gone out into the world.
- 1 John 4:1 (NKJV)

The ability to discern spirits is given by God through His Holy Spirit. We read in 1 Corinthians 12:8-10;

For to one is given the word of wisdom through the Spirit, to another the word of knowledge through the same Spirit, to another faith by the same Spirit, to another gifts of healings by the same Spirit, to another the working of miracles, to another prophecy, to another discerning of spirits...
- 1 Corinthians 12:8-10 (NKJV)

While the ability to discern spirits can be a gift of the Holy Spirit, it is also a skill that is cultivated as we grow in our relationship with God. Just as we learn human languages by association or training, we can also learn to communicate and hear from God by fostering an intimate relationship with Him and by training.

Pitfalls To Watch Out For In The Process Of Recognizing The Voice Of God;

• Hearing from God once does not necessarily mean hearing from God always. Some people may hear from God once and when then mistakenly believe that every of their thought, dreams, vision are from God.

• Your thoughts, emotions and desires can

mislead or influence what you receive spiritually. Strong emotions and thoughts such as anger, love, hatred, passion can cause strong impression in minds and hearts making people believe that they are hearing from God.

• God does not contradict what He has said in the past.

• God will not send you a new message to break His own laws that are established in the scriptures.

• God does not speak only to a certain race of people or certain local language. Many are erroneously teaching that God only speaks to certain race people using it to promote a subtle form of racism and segregation.

• Beware of false leaders and teachers who claim that God spoke to them. There is no way to empirically verify the claim.

• Demons can speak to people making them believe that they have heard from God. Beware of demonic influences.

CHAPTER 7

SYMBOLS, IMAGES AND METAPHORS

"Because it has been given to you to know the mysteries of the kingdom of heaven, but to them it has not been given..."
– Matthew 13:11 (NKJV)

We understand that God speaks to people in many ways. He speaks to us in our local languages but also in the universal language of symbols, images, proverbs and parables. As mentioned earlier, there is a need to have a good understanding of cultural and historical contexts to begin to make sense of what we hear from God.

Below are a few symbols appearing in messages in the Bible. Do personal research to see how much you understand of these symbols or images. Context is very important in understanding symbols, images or parables, and this means that some symbols do not have absolute definitions or meanings in all circumstances. Let us consider two examples of symbols or images in the Bible which can be in a message you receive from God, either appearing in a vision, dream or other sources.

Example 1

Sword (Associated meanings: Divine authority and power, spiritual warfare, judgment and justice, division and separation)

The symbol of the sword conveys various meanings in the Bible and many cultural contexts. In the Bible and in many cultures, it is a tool for executing judgement, justice and punishment (Ezekiel 21:9-11) and can depict divine authority and power. It also carries a connotation of physical or spiritual warfare. Jesus used the symbol as meaning division or separation when he said "Do not think that I came to bring peace on earth. I did not come to bring peace but a sword" (Matthew 10:34), he then goes on to say that families and societies will be divided because of the sword (his word or message).

The Bible also shows us the image of the word of God as the 'Sword of the Spirit' which is 'living and active', sharper than any two-edged sword, that is able to judge thoughts and hearts and enforce change.

If a person receives a message from God that has to do with a sword, the meaning will not be far from any of these concepts but the actual interpretation will depend on the context of the message; for example, was the person given the sword? Was it taken away from him or her? Was it used on someone? etc.

Example 2

Tree (Associated meanings: life, growth, stability, wisdom, a person, and community)

Trees in the bible represents various aspects of life, stability and growth as they provide shelter, shade, sustenance and healing to humans and animals. The Bible conveys the image of trees as persons or communities. In interpreting Nebuchadnezzar's dream in the book of Daniel Chapter 4, Daniel tells the King regarding the tree which he saw in his dream:

> *"It is you, O king, who have grown and become strong; for your greatness has grown and reaches to the heavens, and your dominion to the end of the earth."*
> *- Daniel 4:20-22 (NKJV).*

The Bible also refers to the people of God as 'Trees of righteousness and the planting of the Lord' (Isaiah 61:3). The righteous are like 'trees planted by the river' (Psalm 1:1-6). We also see a description of the Israelites in the wilderness as cedar trees planted by the Lord (Numbers 24:6).

If a person receives a message about trees in a vision or dream, or any other way, the meaning may not be far from the concept of a person, community, growth, stability, healing etc., but the actual meaning and interpretation will depend on the context.

There are words below which are symbolic and I encourage you to write into the spaces provided, what these symbols could mean spiritually in a dream, vision, prophecy etc. and check the Bible for various contexts and inspirations. You can ask other people about what they think the concepts mean spiritually. Also make your own list of many other words that are not included here and researching them to help you grow in understanding the universal spiritual language of symbols.

Remember that recognizing and understanding what God is saying is a journey, the more you learn the better you get at it.

Research what these words mean in the spirit:

Oils (Olive oil, etc.)

____

Goat:

____

Sheep:

____

Gold:

____

Gun:

____

Eagle:

____

Bull / Cow:

____

Human with wings:

____

Vehicles (bicycles, car, aero plane, etc.):

____

Water:

____

Snake:

____

Monkey:

____

Mountain:

____

Make a list of other items or symbols you have seen
or been told spiritually and find out what they mean.

Unlocking Delayed Blessings

By Anthony Esenwa

The book explores the promises of God; What he has promised us, who can claim them, why God's promises can sometimes look unfulfilled and how to take the blessings.

It notes that some doors will never open no matter how hard one knocks on them, if one does not have the key all effort will amount to a waste time and energy. Situations in life can be like those doors; one may cry, shout, moan, beg or curry favour they will not open if one does not have the keys or know the right things to do. The author shares some of the keys needed to open some of life's doors in other to access delayed blessings and promises.